The Royal Chopper

Written by
Cath Jones

Illustrated by
Leo Trinidad

This is Sue. She is the royal chopper.

Her job is to chop down trees in the royal wood.

Dear Sue
I need a big wooden statue of King Jamal for his birthday. Can you do it? We enjoy all the carvings we have from you. They are such good value!
King Gilroy

On Monday, Sue got a royal letter.

Sue set off into the wood. Soon she spotted a big tree. It was a good tree for a statue.

Chip, chop! Chip, chop!
Sue cut down the tree.

But the birds in the wood were not filled with joy!

"We liked sitting in that tree," they moaned. "People need to stop cutting down trees!"

Sue took the tree to the royal garden.

But an owl was still sitting in the tree. Sue did not spot the owl.

All the birds in the wood twittered and flapped.

"We must rescue Owl!" they said.

But how? What was the best thing to do? Wings flapped and feet stamped as the birds argued.

"Let's just go to the royal garden," said a big blue jay. "Then we will see what we can do."

In the garden, King Gilroy was waiting.

"Sue!" he said. "Will you join us for supper? King Jamal is getting some oysters."

Owl pricked up his ears. "Oysters!" he muttered. "Yum! I like oysters!"

Just then, all the rescue birds fluttered into the garden.

They landed on the tree!

Then ... Crash! The tree fell down!
What a mess it all was!

Just then, King Jamal turned up. He had supper with him.

"Ahoy!" he said. "I bring oysters."

The birds spotted the oysters. So did Owl.
As quick as a flash ...
Lick! Munch! Gulp! Burp!
They enjoyed **all** the birthday oysters!

Now Sue and the kings had no oysters for supper!
And King Jamal had no birthday statue.

But King Jamal just grinned.

"Birds need trees to sit in," he said. "So we will plant lots of trees for all the birds in the wood."

"But they will eat oysters just when it is my birthday!"